U.S. Fire Administration

The Seasonal Nature of Fires

January 2005

 FEMA

FA-236
January 2005

United States Fire Administration/National Fire Data Center

The Seasonal Nature of Fires

Department of Homeland Security
Federal Emergency Management Agency
United States Fire Administration
National Fire Data Center

U.S. Fire Administration Mission Statement

As an entity of the Federal Emergency Management Agency, the mission of the United States Fire Administration is to reduce life and economic losses due to fire and related emergencies through leadership, advocacy, coordination, and support. We serve the Nation independently, in coordination with other Federal agencies and in partnership with fire protection and emergency service communities. With a commitment to excellence, we provide public education, training, technology, and data initiatives.

On March 1, 2003, FEMA became part of the U.S. Department of Homeland Security. FEMA's continuing mission within the new department is to lead the effort to prepare the Nation for all hazards and effectively manage Federal response and recovery efforts following any national incident. FEMA also initiates proactive mitigation activities, trains first responders, and manages the Citizen Corps, the National Flood Insurance Program, and the U.S. Fire Administration.

CONTENTS

LIST OF FIGURES

LIST OF TABLES

THE SEASONAL NATURE OF FIRES

Executive Summary

As weather and human activities change with the seasons of the year, so does the incidence, causes and severity of fires. Cold winter weather increases indoor activities and the need for heating, which brings about the peak period of heating structure fires. Daily fire incidence is at its highest in the spring. Spring is characterized by an increase in outside fires and a decrease in fires related to heating. The increase in outside spring fires is in large part due to the increase in tree, grass, and brush fires. Summer fires reflect an increase of incendiary and suspicious fires, fires associated with fireworks and natural fires caused by lightning strikes. These fires are a reflection of the change to warmer weather and the consequent increase in both outside activities and dry natural vegetation. Fire incidence is at its lowest in the fall. In fall, there is a decrease in outside fires, an increase in heating-related structure fires and the peak period of cooking fires. The incidence of vehicle fires is relatively constant throughout the year, as are their causes.

The incidence of daily fires increases during and around four holiday periods: Independence Day, Halloween, Thanksgiving, and the winter holiday period that includes Christmas and New Year's. More fires are reported on July 4th than any other day of the year. Brush and outside fires increase substantially due to family outings and the misuse of fireworks. On Halloween, and the night before, incendiary and suspicious structure fires are about 60 percent more frequent than on an average day. As might be expected, cooking fires increase on both Thanksgiving and Christmas days, but drop below average on the following days. In addition to Christmas, the winter holidays include Hanukkah, Kwanzaa, and New Year's. During this period, structure fires increase and the dollar loss per fire is 34 percent greater than normal, due largely to the decorative use of Christmas trees, other combustible materials such as wrapping paper, and candles. Alcohol may also play a contributing role in the increase in holiday fires.

Introduction

Nearly 1.7 million fires in the United States during 2002 claimed 3,380 lives, injured 18,425 people, and destroyed over $10 billion in property.[1] Incendiary and suspicious acts (including arson), cooking and carelessness with open flames are the leading causes of fires.[2] These causes have a common thread: human activity and human error. As such, most of these fires were likely preventable.

Many activities that influence fire incidence change with the season of the year. In the winter, the need for heating increases. Hot, dry weather affects wildland areas and creates fire-prone situations. Warm weather tends to bring people and their behaviors outdoors. Behaviors also change as people participate in various holiday customs and traditions. At some holidays, decorations in the home increase the load of combustible material. The use of candles and extra

---

[1] *Fire Loss in the United States 2002*, National Fire Protection Association.

[2] National Fire Incident Reporting System (NFIRS), U.S. Fire Administration, 2001–2002 average.

electric lighting may be used to celebrate other events. Fireworks are part of Fourth of July and other celebrations. As part of seasonal celebrations, people may prepare and cook elaborate meals. People also travel more, leaving some homes unoccupied while other homes increase in occupancy.

Any of these behaviors can affect both the incidence and the severity of fires. By understanding the nature and scope of seasonal fires, public education and other fire-related programs can be specifically targeted at these seasonal fire problems.

This report first explores fire patterns by each season of the year; both the changes in incidence and the causes of fire are discussed. The report then focuses on the changes in fire profiles around four seasonal holidays: Independence Day, Halloween, Thanksgiving, and Christmas. These holidays were chosen because of their striking changes in fire patterns.

Methods

The findings in this report are based primarily on evaluation of two years of National Fire Incident Reporting System (NFIRS) fire incident data (2001–2002).[3] NFIRS is a voluntary data collection system administered by the United States Fire Administration (USFA), a division of the Federal Emergency Management Agency (FEMA). In 2002, 13,894 fire departments in 49 states submitted data to NFIRS. The participating fire departments include career, volunteer, and combination departments that serve communities ranging from rural hamlets to the largest cities. Participation in NFIRS is voluntary, so fire incidents that are reported may not reflect all of a department's activity. Also, information that is recorded for an incident is not required to be complete. Nevertheless, each year of NFIRS data contains between 600,000 and 800,000 records, each representing a separate fire report. This makes NFIRS the largest fire database in the world.

The data used in this report were averaged over 2001 and 2002. Two years of data were used to smooth out fluctuations or anomalies that may arise in any single year. These fluctuations may be caused by any of a number of factors, such as climatological effects (e.g., a cold winter, a dry summer), changes in demographics (e.g., increasing or decreasing population), or changes in reporting.

A second resource used in compiling the data is the annual National Fire Protection Association (NFPA) survey of municipal fire departments. Each year, the NFPA receives about 3,000 responses to their survey. Departments are randomly selected, with the sampling stratified by size of the community that participated. The NFPA extrapolates statistics from the survey to estimate total annual fire loss in the United States. These statistics include total dollar loss, injuries, fatalities, and fire incidence. Applying the percentage of reported loss from an NFIRS category to the total loss estimated by the NFPA provides an estimate of the national loss for a specific category of fire incidents. This procedure was used in this study to estimate fire incidence, total dollar loss, and casualties and is the accepted methodology for fire-related data analyses.

---

[3]At the writing of this report, NFIRS is continuing to transition from Version 4.1 to 5.0. Some Version 4.1 data elements do not convert directly to Version 5.0, therefore only incidents reported in Version 5.0 were used in this report. Additionally, mutual aid records were excluded from analysis. The seasonal analysis is based on over 685,000 Version 5.0 incidents, or 57 percent of all reported fire incidents during 2001 and 2002.

Adjusted Percentages

In making national estimates, the unknowns in the database should not be ignored. The approach taken in this report is to provide an "adjusted" percentage that is computed using only those incidents for which the cause was provided. In effect, this distributes the fires for which the cause is unknown in the same proportion as the fires for which the cause is known, which may or may not be approximately right.

Seasonal Fire Profile

For purposes of this report, winter is defined as the months of January through March, spring as April through June, summer as July through September and fall as October through December. Seasons are not as specific nor as easily defined as other fire factors. Climatic changes associated with seasons are not well bounded. Although defined by calendar dates of solstices and equinoxes, seasons actually blend into one another and produce climates that differ by area of the country. Yearly weather changes affect the seasonal variations and flow as well as human activities. Nevertheless, even with some blurring, seasons do have characteristic fire profile tendencies. These characteristics may be the result of climatic changes in concert with seasonal differences in human activities.

Average temperatures in 2001 and 2002 were the sixth and fourteenth warmest years on record, respectively, for the United States. Globally, 2001 was the second warmest year on record. During November 2001, two-thirds of the country was considered "very warm," within the top ten percent of recorded temperatures for that month. From 1999 through 2001 the country experienced below average precipitation levels. The states most affected were along the coasts (Maine had its driest year on record) while states from the upper Midwest southward along the Mississippi River Valley received above normal precipitation. From January through October 2001, 15 to 20 percent of the country experienced long term drought considered to be extreme or severe. The 2001–2002 winter season was the ninth warmest on record, and particularly warm in the Northwest. Summer 2002 was tied for the third warmest in 108 years, although temperatures cooled toward historic averages in the fall. During 2002 drought conditions generally improved in the eastern U.S., although the drought worsened in much of the western half of the country and the central and southern Great Lakes.[4]

Averaged over 2 years, the seasonal nature of fire becomes more evident (Figure 1). For example, the number of fires in winter is much less than summer. Some interesting spikes on particular days were evident; the highest by far is July 4. Forty-five percent of reported annual fires were outside fires, so much of the overall seasonal fire pattern not surprisingly is a result of the variation in outside fires. Daily incidence of outside fires were most numerous in the spring, structure fires increase in the colder months, and vehicle fires were fairly constant throughout the year (Figure 2). Because vehicle fires show only a slight seasonal variation in incidence and cause of fire, the focus of this report is primarily on outside fires and structure fires.

---

[4]National Oceanic and Atmospheric Administration (NOAA) National Climatic Data Center Web site http://www.ncdc.noaa.gov.

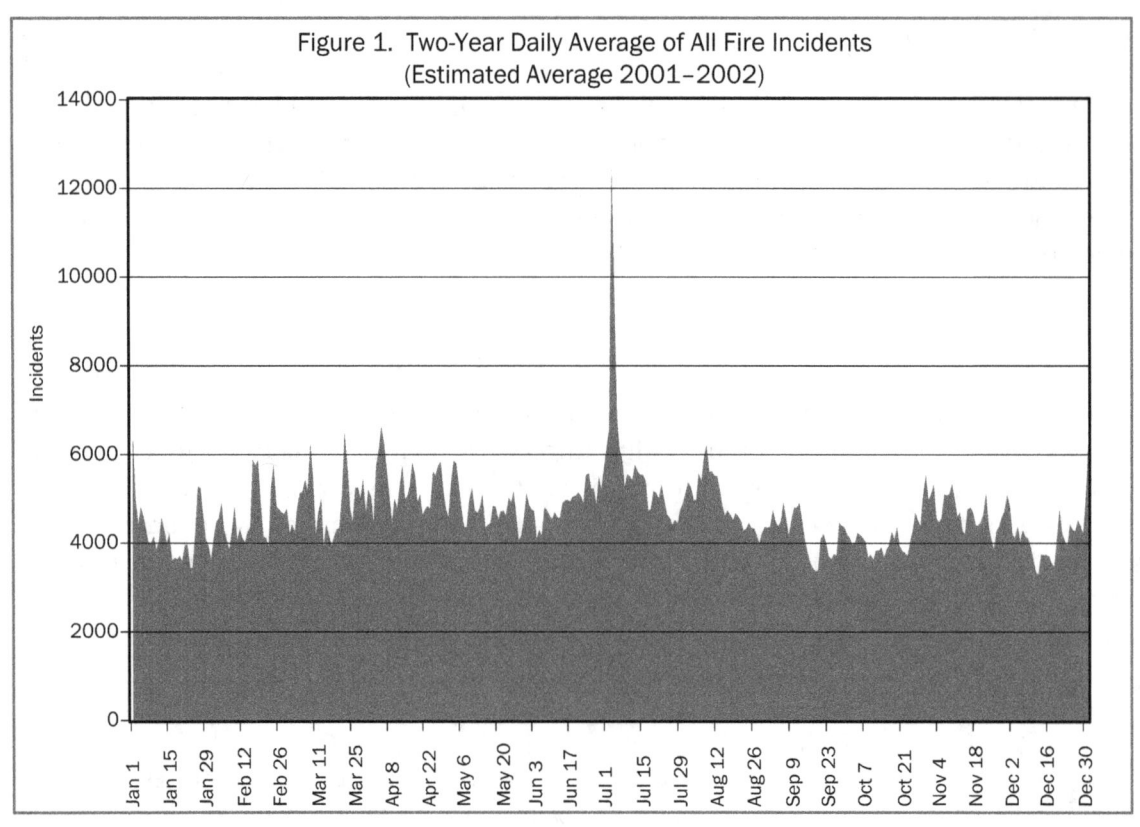

Figure 1. Two-Year Daily Average of All Fire Incidents
(Estimated Average 2001–2002)

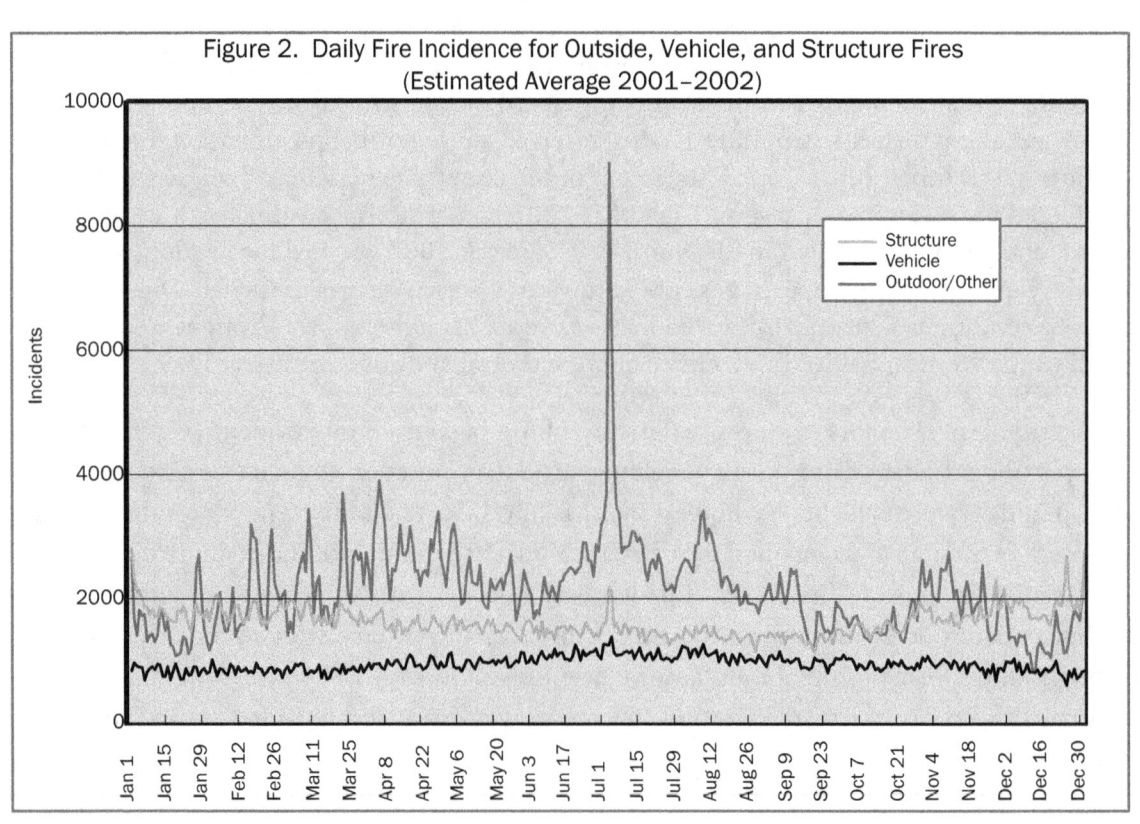

Figure 2. Daily Fire Incidence for Outside, Vehicle, and Structure Fires
(Estimated Average 2001–2002)

On average, spring finds heightened fire incidence with a seasonal average of nearly 5,000 fires each day (Table 1). The increase in fires begins in the late winter and continues through the summer. Winter fires, even with the extra amount associated with residential heating, occur less often (4,548 fires each day) because of the drop in outside fires and vehicle fires. Summer fires, including the spike in fires during the July 4th festivities, rank second in incidence, or 4,932 fires per day. Fire incidence is at its lowest in the fall at 4,285 incidents each day, a 14 percent decrease from the spring.

Table 1. Daily Incidence of Fires by Month and Season
(estimated average 2001–2002)

Season	Month	Daily Average	Daily Seasonal Average
Winter	January	4,203	
	February	4,604	4,548
	March	4,842	
Spring	April	5,291	
	May	4,787	4,986
	June	4,886	
Summer	July	5,683	
	August	4,897	4,932
	September	4,191	
Fall	October	4,103	
	November	4,664	4,285
	December	4,101	

Over the year, incendiary and suspicious fires were the most common cause of fire. They account for 22 percent of all fires on average (Figure 3). Incendiary and suspicious fires were proportionally lower in the fall and winter than in the spring and summer, and were the lead cause in each season except fall. Cooking increases substantially in the fall, due in part to holiday cooking, and is the second leading cause of fires in all other seasons.

Winter

In the winter, structure fires increase, although total fires decrease. A substantial portion of the structure fire increase is caused by heating fires (Figure 4). In an average year, heating is the cause of 17 percent of structure fires; however, during the winter, heating fires jump to 27 percent of structure fires. Heating fires were concentrated in late fall through mid winter (December–February) during winter holidays and the coldest months. Since colder temperatures result in longer operating time for heating equipment, there is more opportunity for that equipment to cause a fire.

Winter also sees an increase in outside fires caused by open flame-fires ignited by matches, open fires (including campfires), and embers. In fact, open flame is the second leading cause of outside winter fires, after incendiary or suspicious fires, possibly the by-product of fires initially lighted for warmth.

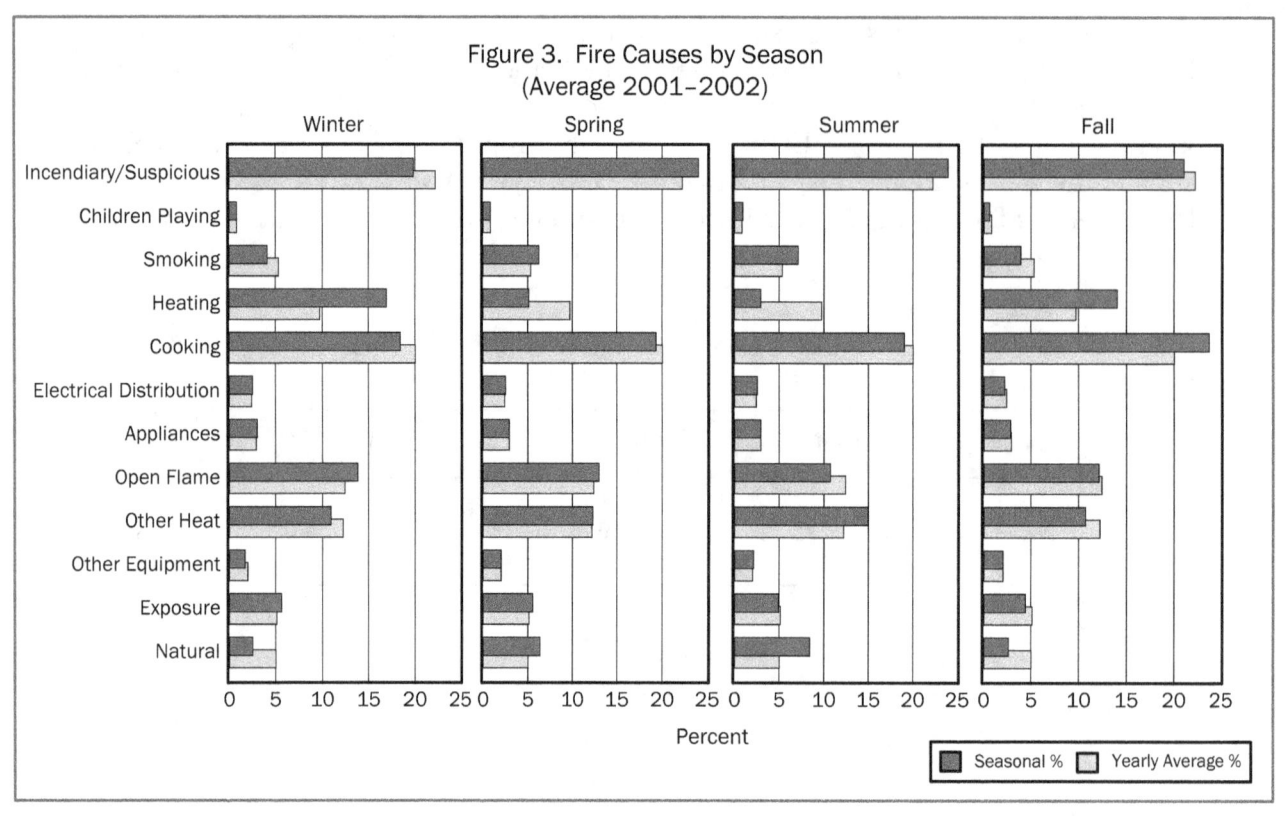

Figure 3. Fire Causes by Season
(Average 2001–2002)

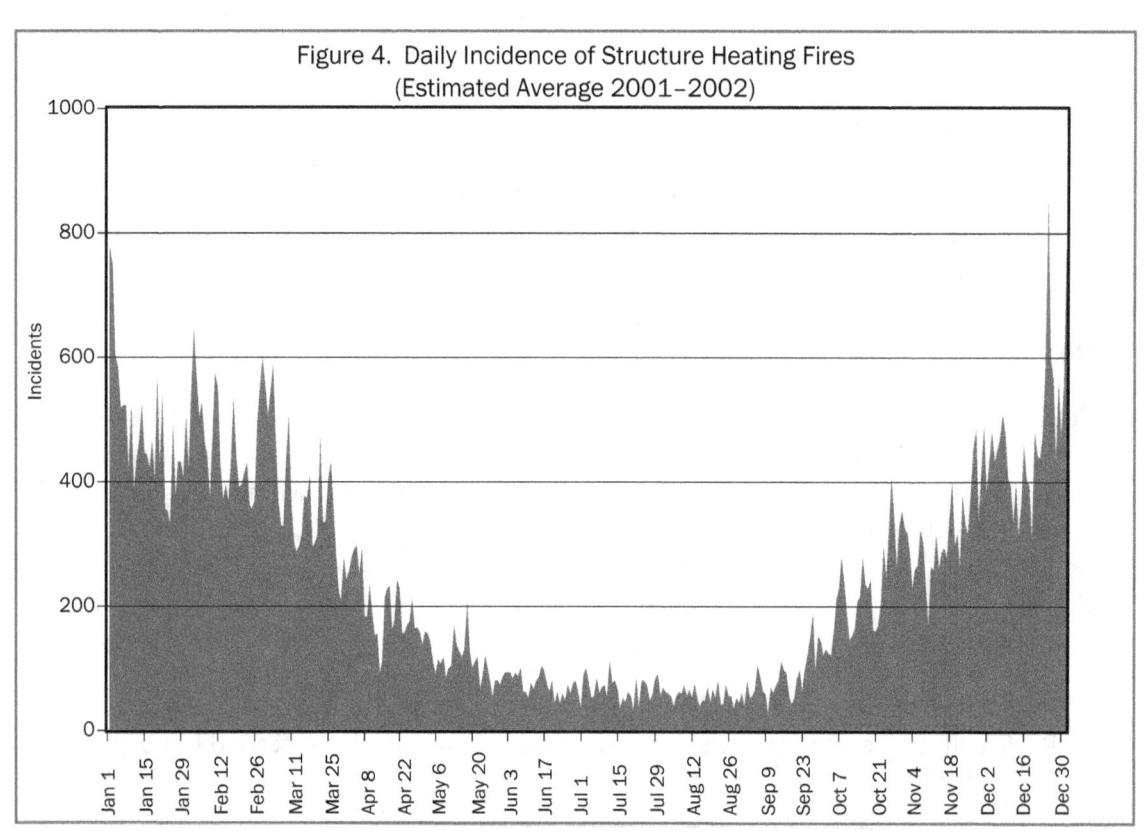

Figure 4. Daily Incidence of Structure Heating Fires
(Estimated Average 2001–2002)

Spring

Spring is the season with the highest daily average of fires. This peak is largely due to an increase in outside fires—especially tree, brush, and grass fires (Figure 5). This increase is generally because relative humidity tends to be lower, winds tend to be higher, and, because leaves are still off trees or just beginning to bud, sunlight can directly reach the ground to both warm and dry surface fuels (such as the previous fall's leaves).[5] Such conditions are favorable for the ignition of dry grass and brush. Although the timing of these conditions may vary from region to region, spring has the highest average daily incidence of outdoor fires, a 17 percent increase over the average. About 30 percent of the reported tree, brush, and grass fires occur within these 3 months.

Incendiary and suspicious fires also peak in the spring. This peak is not surprising as 55 percent of overall incendiary and suspicious fires were outside fires. Heating fires decline in structures in spring, as expected, while cooking fires begin to increase. Wildland fires—the subset of tree, brush, and grass fires that occur in Wildland areas—increase to about 44 fires per day in the spring.[6]

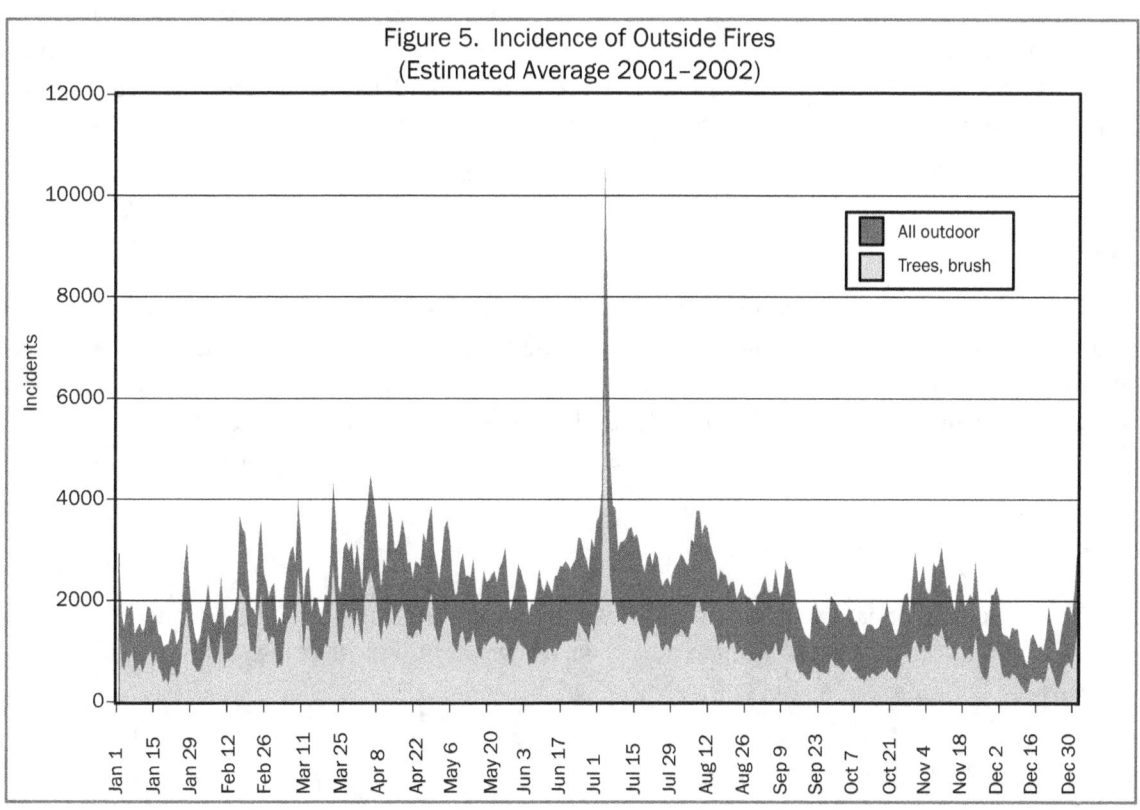

Figure 5. Incidence of Outside Fires (Estimated Average 2001–2002)

---

[5]Virginia Department of Forestry, http://www.dof.virginia.gov/fire/va-fire-history.shtml accessed December 2004.

[6]Wildland fires are identified as NFIRS Incident Type 140–143 and Property Use 669. These are forests with and without logging operations. They include wildlife preserves; timber tracts used to plant, replant, and conserve forests; and timber and log piles in forests. Wildland fires do not include fires in sawmills operating in the forest.

Summer

The predictable peak of fires around July 4 is due to an increase in grass and brush fires ignited by fireworks. Many fires set by fireworks go unreported, so the peak is undoubtedly much sharper than shown in Figure 5. Following this holiday, summer fire incidence steadily declines. Fires caused by natural phenomenon (Figure 6) follow a similar pattern of increasing incidence during summer. Lightning strikes are highest in the summer, which is often the cause of natural fires. The dangers from summer lightning are compounded with potentially dry conditions and high temperatures that contribute to the rapid spread of wildfire during the summer and early fall.

Figure 7 shows the estimated daily incidence of all fires caused by open flame. This includes fires started by matches, lighters, embers, and torches.[7] Contrary to popular belief, the incidence of outside fires caused by open flame is lower during the summer than the winter and spring. The decline begins in the summer and continues through the fall. The reduction of open flame fires in the summer is countered by the increase in fires caused by natural phenomena, other heat sources, and other equipment.

Incendiary/suspicious is the leading cause of summer fires, causing nearly one quarter of all fires. Cooking is the leading cause of structure fires in the summer and the second leading cause of fires overall. Children playing fires peak in summer. Heating fires account for only 6 percent of summer structure fires, but the reduction in heating fires is offset by increases in nearly all other causes.

Fall

Fire incidence is at its lowest level in the fall months. The weather is still mild, so structure heating has not become a dominant factor. Cooking is the leading cause of both structure fires and fires overall during the fall; incendiary and suspicious fires were the leading cause of outside fires. Outside fires decline in the fall, reaching their lowest point in the late fall. The proportion of fires caused by open flame increases in the fall from its summer low.

Holiday Fire Profile

The incidence of daily fires increase during and around four nationally celebrated holidays. This section details the 2-year average of loss data surrounding these holidays and explores the reasons for the increase in fires.

Independence Day

In all years studied, Independence Day has more incidents reported in NFIRS than any other day of the year (see Figure 1). The number of incidents in the NFIRS database associated

---

[7]The cause "open flame" is a residual category that includes fires started by torches, matches, lighters, candles, open fires (e.g., campfires, bonfires, warning flares, rubbish fires, open trash burners, open incinerators, outdoor fireplaces), hot embers, ashes, and rekindles. Open flame fires are not associated with fires caused by arson, children playing, smoking, heating, cooking, electrical distribution, or appliances.

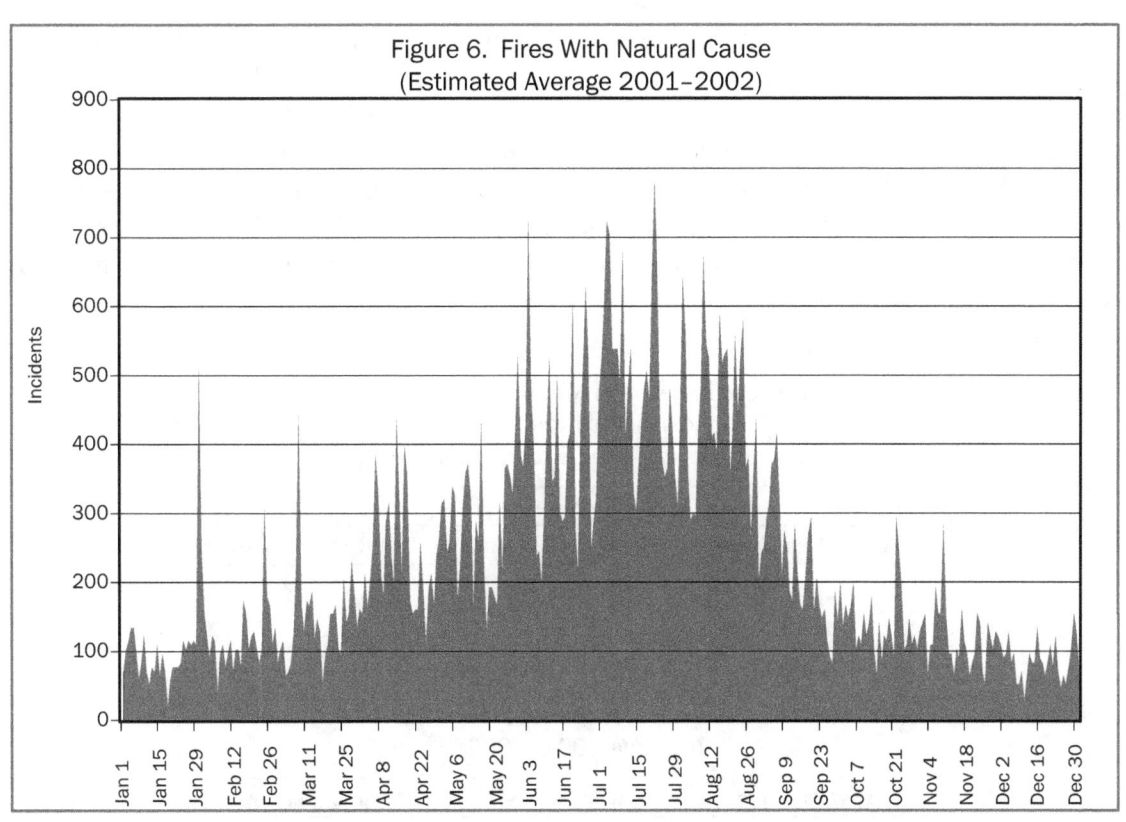

Figure 6. Fires With Natural Cause
(Estimated Average 2001–2002)

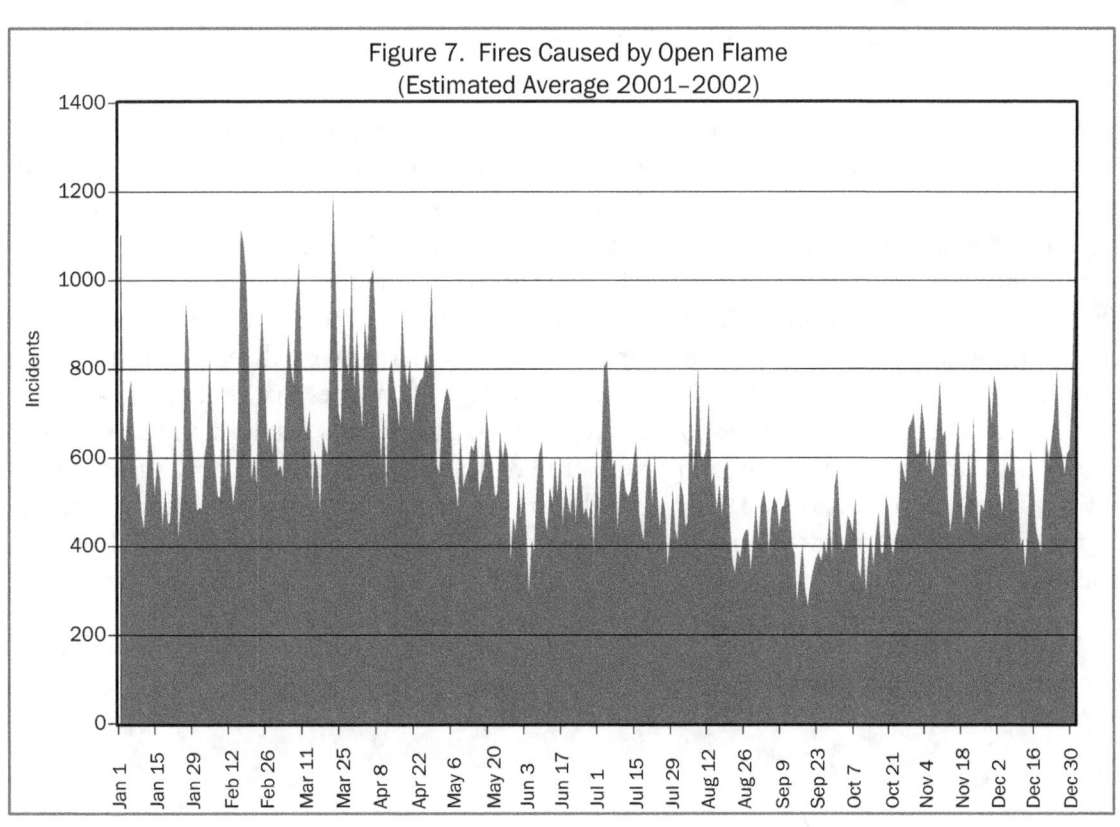

Figure 7. Fires Caused by Open Flame
(Estimated Average 2001–2002)

with July 4 and July 5 were 2.4 times the average daily number of incidents on other days of the year (Table 2). Brush and outside fire incidents were nearly four times higher during this holiday than on the average day. Structure fires increase on July 4 and July 5th as well. As would be expected, fireworks were responsible for a considerable portion of the increase in fire incidence on Independence Day. In fact, 31 percent of the total annual number of fireworks-related fires occur on July 4 and 5. As shown in Table 3, however, these fires individually were less severe than fires generally, with lower average dollar loss per fire, less than half of the injuries and one third the deaths per fire.

Table 2. Relative Increase in Number of Reported Incidents
by Selected Incident Type for July 4 and 5
(ratio of total for July 4 and 5 to total for average day)

Year	Relative Increase			
	All Incidents	Fireworks	Structures	Outside Fires
2001	2.4	58.4	1.3	3.9
2002	2.4	55.1	1.3	3.7

Table 3. Loss Measures Per Fire for Independence Day Fires
(average 2001–2002)

Loss Measure	Average Day	July 4 and 5 (per day)
Dollar Loss/Incident	$6,245	$3,581
Injuries/1,000 Incidents	12.7	5.90
Fatalities/1,000 Incidents	2.5	0.79

Although losses per fire incident were not high, the sheer volume of incidents on July 4 and 5 results in an increase in the total number of casualties. Each year, between 8,000 and 9,000 individuals require emergency room treatment for fireworks-related injuries. Many other fireworks injuries are treated at home. Based on a survey of hospitals, the U.S. Consumer Product Safety Commission (CPSC) estimated 9,500 injuries from fireworks in 2001 and 8,800 in 2002.[8] The CPSC reports that approximately 5,700 of these injuries occurred during the month of July in both years. Many burn and fire injuries, particularly those that result from fireworks, do not appear in the NFIRS database. Instead, only injuries that result from a fire to which the local fire department responds is reported to NFIRS. As a result, if an individual is injured with fireworks but no fire requiring a fire department response occurs, the incident will not appear in fire incident data, even if the fire department was the emergency medical service (EMS) first responder. Thus, the fire injury data understate the true magnitude of the problem.

Total annual dollar loss for fires on July 4 and 5 is estimated to be at least $77 million for both property loss and loss of contents.

---

[8]Greene, Michael A. and James Joholske, 2000 Fireworks Annual Report: Fireworks-Related Deaths, Emergency Department Treated Injuries, and Enforcement Activities During 2002, U.S. Consumer Product Safety Commission, June 2003.

Fireworks are not the only cause of Independence Day fires. Independence Day is a traditional opportunity to engage in outdoor activities, such as family picnics. Many brush and other outside fires result from the misuse of heat of ignition, which includes abandoned and discarded materials, inadequate control of an open fire, and children playing with the heat source. Activities that require the use of an open flame are particular culprits—the lighting of barbecues, the match used to light fireworks, improperly discarded charcoal ashes, or children playing with heat sources (perhaps fireworks or grilling materials).

The causes of fires on July 4 and 5 differ in several important areas from the rest of the year (Figure 8). The proportion of fires caused by other heat, fires of incendiary and suspicious origin and fires caused by children playing were substantially higher on July 4 than both the summer and the annual averages. (Fireworks fires are classified under "other heat, ember, and spark"; hence, the dramatic increase in that category.) Independence Day injuries can be reduced with proper supervision of children and preventing them from gaining access to lighters, matches, and other dangerous items, including fireworks. Because children tend to emulate adults, adults should apply safe practices while cooking outdoors and handling legal fireworks.

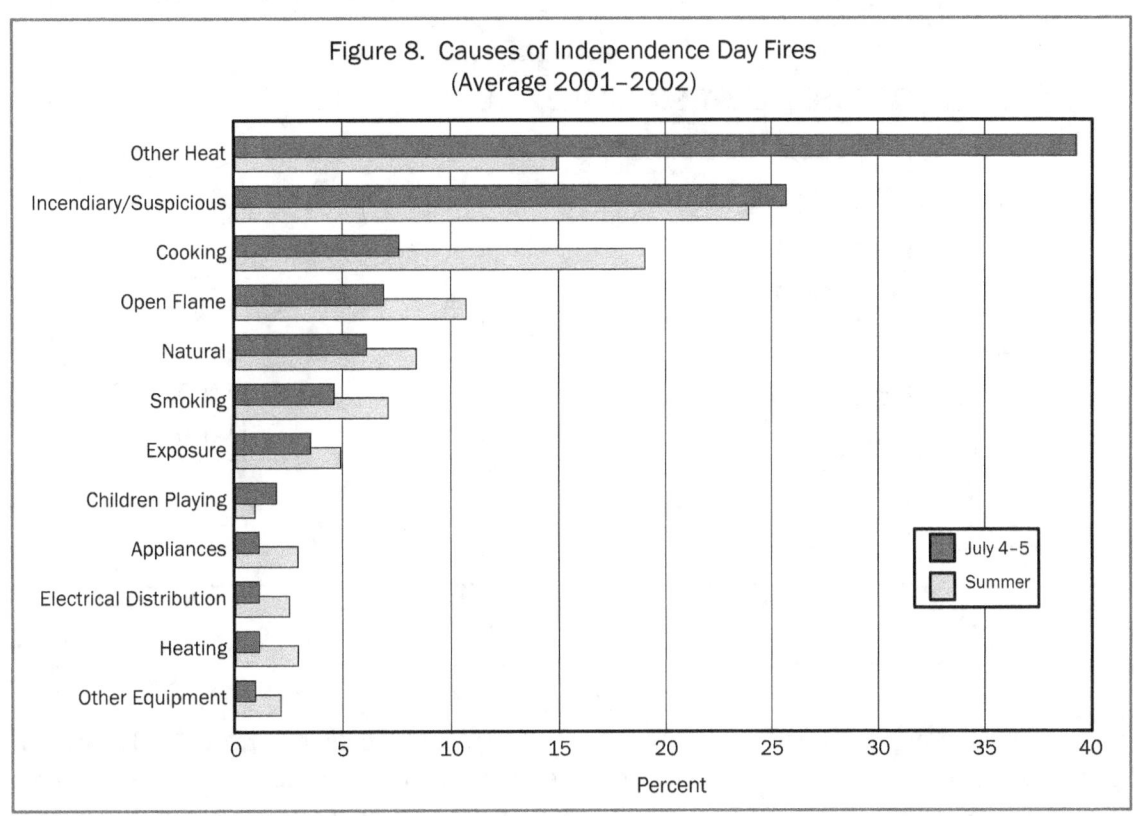

Figure 8. Causes of Independence Day Fires
(Average 2001–2002)

There is no clear explanation for the proportional increase of incendiary and suspicious fires on Independence Day; perhaps excesses of celebrating and the opportunity for vandalism and mischief contribute to the increase. Regardless of the root cause, these data serve as a warning that fireworks-related fires or other Independence Day fires are not all accidental. In fact, of the more than 6,600 incendiary and suspicious fires on July 4 and 5, the form of heat of ignition was fireworks 32 percent of the time and matches 21 percent of the time. Twenty eight percent of the incendiary and suspicious fires on these dates had wood or paper as the type of material first ignited, 19 percent were fabric or textiles, 15 percent were natural products (e.g., grass, leaves, hay, straw, tobacco, rubber, grain, coal).

Halloween and "Devil's Night"

Halloween, including the so-called "Devil's Night" the night before, is another holiday when fires spike, although considerably less sharply than the July 4 peak. This is true for both outside and structure fires. As Halloween has been typically associated with activities and cultural icons related to mischief, it is not surprising to find that the origin of many of these fires is suspicious or incendiary (Figure 9).

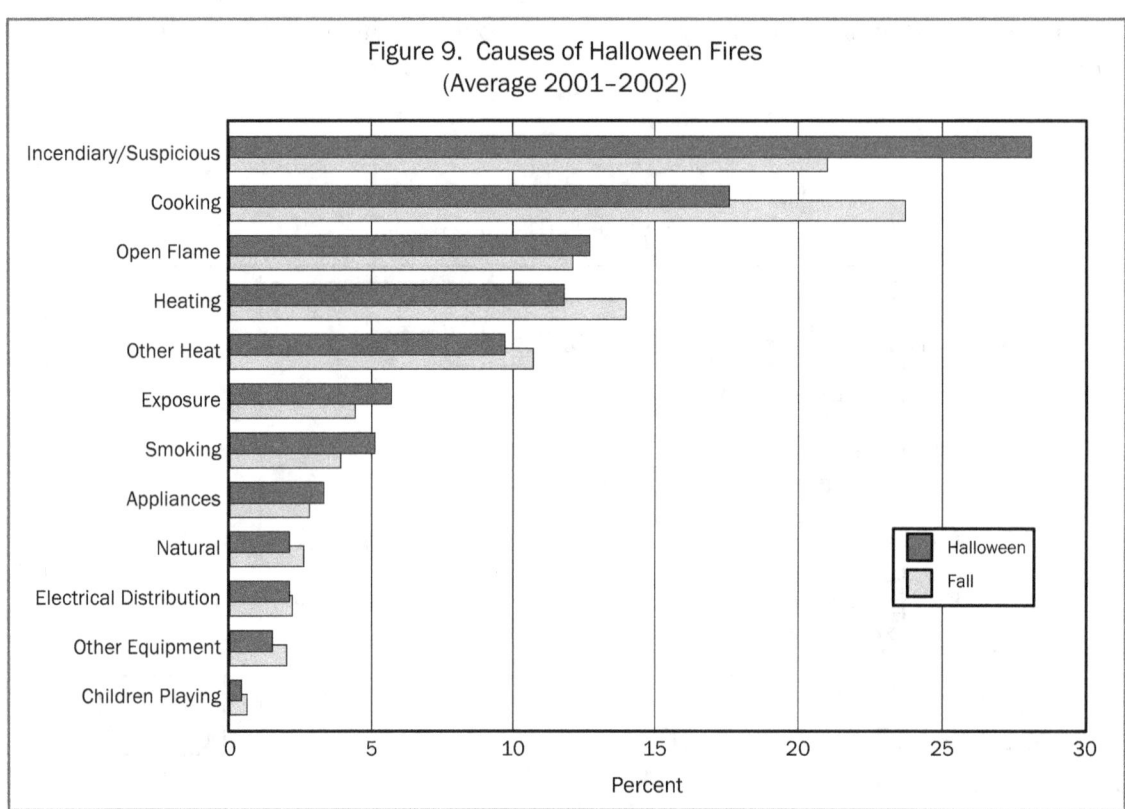

The day and night of Devil's Night (October 30) had a 59 percent increase and Halloween (October 31) had a 63 percent increase in the daily occurrence of incendiary or suspicious structure fires (Figure 10) for October and November. As seen in Figure 11, the peak in incendiary and suspicious structure fires on Halloween is slightly lower than the peak on July 5th but higher than New Year's Day. Though Devil's Night arson fires occur more frequently than other nights, the trend has decreased from previous years. Public awareness of Devil's Night has played a role in this reduction of arson.

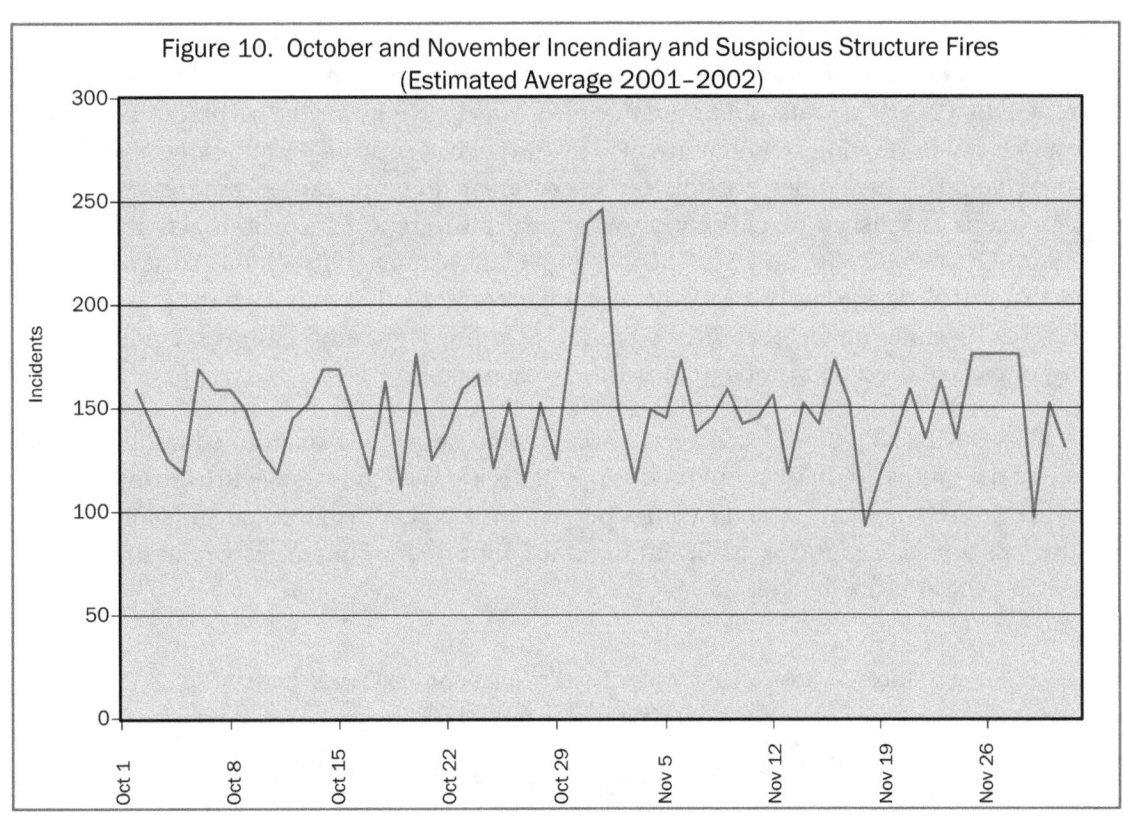

Figure 10. October and November Incendiary and Suspicious Structure Fires
(Estimated Average 2001–2002)

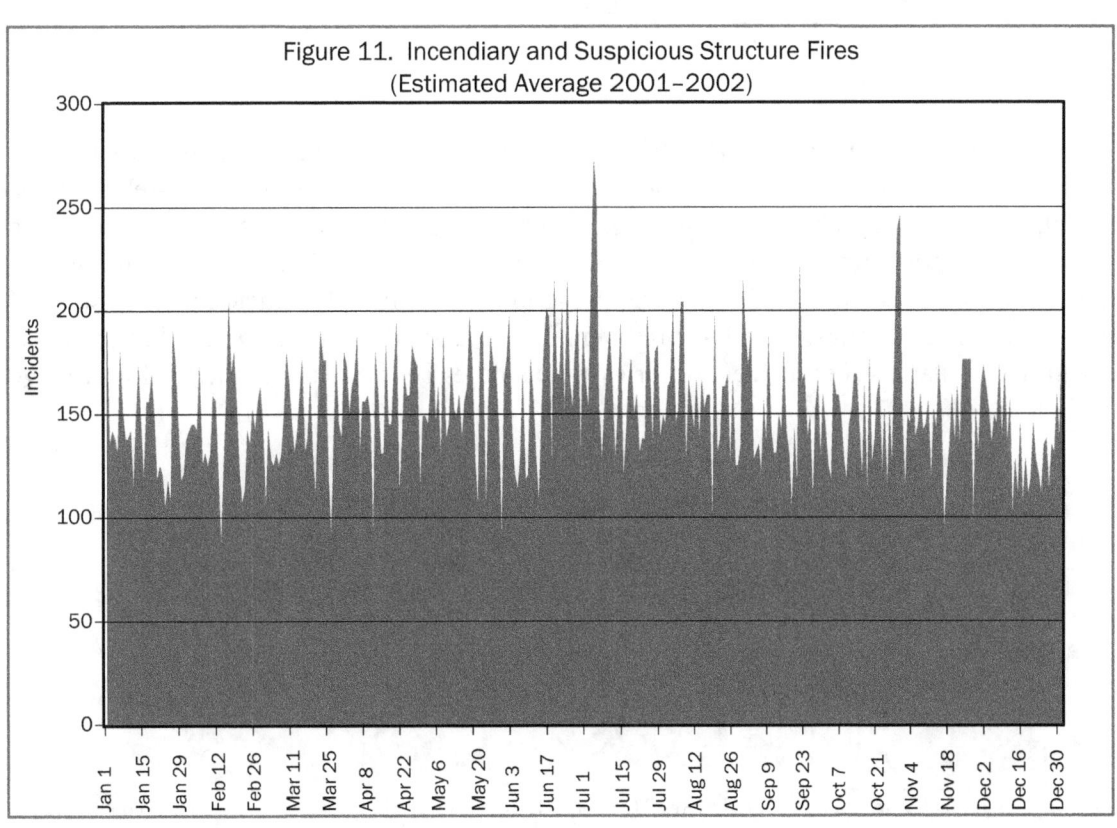

Figure 11. Incendiary and Suspicious Structure Fires
(Estimated Average 2001–2002)

13

In Detroit, where the problem was especially severe in the 1990's, a special effort has been made over several years to combat the incidence of arson on Devil's Night. Police and city officials credit a nearly decade-old program called Angel's Night for the turnaround in arson activity. The city involved the community in activities such as securing or removing abandoned buildings, vehicles, and other possible targets of arson (e.g., discarded mattresses, trash). Detroit citizens established neighborhood watch patrols to report suspicious activity around the city on October 29, 30, and 31. The city provides flashing yellow lights to some watch groups that patrol via automobile. Detroit, along with several other municipalities, established a curfew for juveniles on October 29, 30, and 31. Curfew legislation has been credited with helping to reduce the arson problem over the 3-day period.[9]

Because Devil's Night and Halloween arson is often targeted at abandoned buildings and vacant lots the estimated dollar property loss per fire is less than the average fire during the rest of the year. Fire-related injuries and fatalities per day were higher than the annual (Table 4). The total fire loss for the 2 nights is estimated to total $56 million. These fires were estimated to injure 136 people and kill about 27.

Table 4. Loss Measures for Devil's Night and Halloween Fires
(average 2001–2002)

Loss Measure	Average Day	Oct. 30–Nov. 1 (per day)
Dollar Loss/Fire	$6,245	$5,360
Injuries/1,000 Fires	12.7	14.4
Fatalities/1,000 Fires	2.5	3.1

Thanksgiving

For many, the family dinner is the highlight of the Thanksgiving holiday.[10] As may be expected, the extensive cooking on Thanksgiving results in numerous cooking-related fires. Indeed, cooking fires peak on Thanksgiving. About 5,200 Thanksgiving Day fires require a fire department response, cause $21 million in property losses, and result in about 51 injuries and 11 fatalities. Of these fires, cooking is the cause in more than 2,200 incidents, or about 43 percent of all fires. Thanksgiving Day fires were less destructive than average day fires, with 32 percent less dollar loss per incident. Injuries and fatalities per fire were slightly below average (Table 5).

Table 5. Loss Measures for All Thanksgiving Day Fires
(average 2001–2002)

Loss Measure	Average	Thanksgiving Day
Dollar Loss/Fire	$6,245	$4,249
Injuries/1,000 Fires	12.7	11.1
Fatalities/1,000 Fires	2.5	2.4

---

[9]"Detroit Neighbors Stamp Out Devil's Night Fires," October 31, 2000, http://www.apbnews.com, accessed November 2000.

[10]The Thanksgiving Days analyzed in this report were Nov. 22, 2001 and Nov. 28, 2002.

It is particularly important to analyze residential structure fires on Thanksgiving, as many families spend the holiday in their home or in the home of a friend or family member. Cooking is the leading cause of residential structure fires on Thanksgiving, followed by heating and open flame. Ovens and cooking ranges were the leading type of equipment involved in Thanksgiving Day residential structure fires. Thanksgiving Day residential structure fires were also less damaging and cause fewer casualties than residential structure fires on other days (Table 6).

Table 6. Loss Measures for Thanksgiving Day Residential Structure Fires
(average 2001–2002)

Loss Measure	Average	Thanksgiving Day
Dollar Loss/Fire	$13,188	$8,054
Injuries/1,000 Fires	35.8	22.9
Fatalities/1,000 Fires	6.9	5.7

Vehicle fires on Thanksgiving substantially decrease. Over the two years studied, the incidence of vehicle fires on Thanksgiving Day decreased 33 percent as compared to the year-round daily average. This may be an indication of reduced vehicle travel on Thanksgiving Day itself.

Winter Holiday Season

The winter holiday season is defined here as being from December 1 to January 7. The winter holiday season exists during a time of elevated risk for winter heating fires and contains several holidays—Hanukkah, Christmas, Kwanzaa, and New Year's—each with the potential to change the profile of fire incidence and cause. Many people begin the celebration of the season by decorating their home with seasonal garlands, electric lights, candles, banners, or displays. Probably the most popular addition for the holiday season, and as fire hazard, is the Christmas tree. It may ignite easily, especially if dried out, it burns vigorously, and it often is positioned in such a way to allow rapid fire spread to other combustible materials in the house. The lights on the tree and proximity to fireplaces add to the danger, along with discarded gift wrapping. The use of candles for decorative or religious purposes also increases during this period.

Christmas and New Year's experienced a substantial increase in structure fires caused by open flame compared to the average day (Table 7). Thanksgiving also had a relative increase in open flame fires although not as pronounced. This increase may be related to the use of candles in seasonal displays.

Table 7. Increase in Structure Open Flame Fires for Selected Holidays
(average 2001–2002)

Date	Relative Increase
Average Day	1.0
New Year's Day	2.1
Halloween	1.0
Thanksgiving	1.3
Christmas	2.4

Winter holiday fires were more severe than the average fire during the year across all loss measures (Table 8). Christmas tree and other decoration fires were substantially more damaging—injuries per fire were twice as high as the average winter holiday fire, fatalities per fire were five times greater and the dollar loss per fire was over three times the winter holiday average. This is indicative of the potential rapid spread of a tree or decoration fire. The rate of Christmas tree fires per day was higher in the last half of December than the first half, and then declined during the first week of January (Table 9).

Table 8. Loss Measures for Winter Holiday Fires: December 1–January 7
(average 2001–2002)

Loss Measure	Average	All Winter Holiday Fires	Christmas Tree and Decoration Fires
Dollar Loss/Fire	$6,245	$7,783	$27,259
Injuries/1,000 Fires	12.7	15.9	39.0
Fatalities/1,000 Fires	2.5	4.2	21.3

Table 9. Christmas Tree Fires in December and Early January
(average 2001–2002)

Period	Christmas Tree Fires/Day
December 1–14	32.7
December 15–31	46.2
January 1–7	42.1

Similar to Thanksgiving Day, there is an increased incidence of cooking fires on Christmas Eve and Christmas Day, while December 26 has fewer cooking fires than an average day of the year (Table 10). Again like Thanksgiving, the incidence of vehicle fires decreases on Christmas. Over the 2-year period, vehicle fires decreased 36 percent on Christmas Day compared to the year-round daily average.

Table 10. Christmas Cooking Fires
(average 2001–2002)

Date	Relative Increase
Average Day	1.0
December 24	1.4
December 25	1.8
December 26	0.9

16

The incidence of fires caused by cooking, heating, and open flame (Figure 12 and Table 5) increases during this period. This is not surprising due to holiday cooking and the more prevalent use of home fireplaces, displays, and decorations involving candles (Figure 13). The daily incidence of candle-started fires nearly quadruples on Christmas Day. One dangerous scenario is that wrappings are thrown near a fireplace, embers fall on the paper, and the Christmas tree or other nearby flammables ignite.

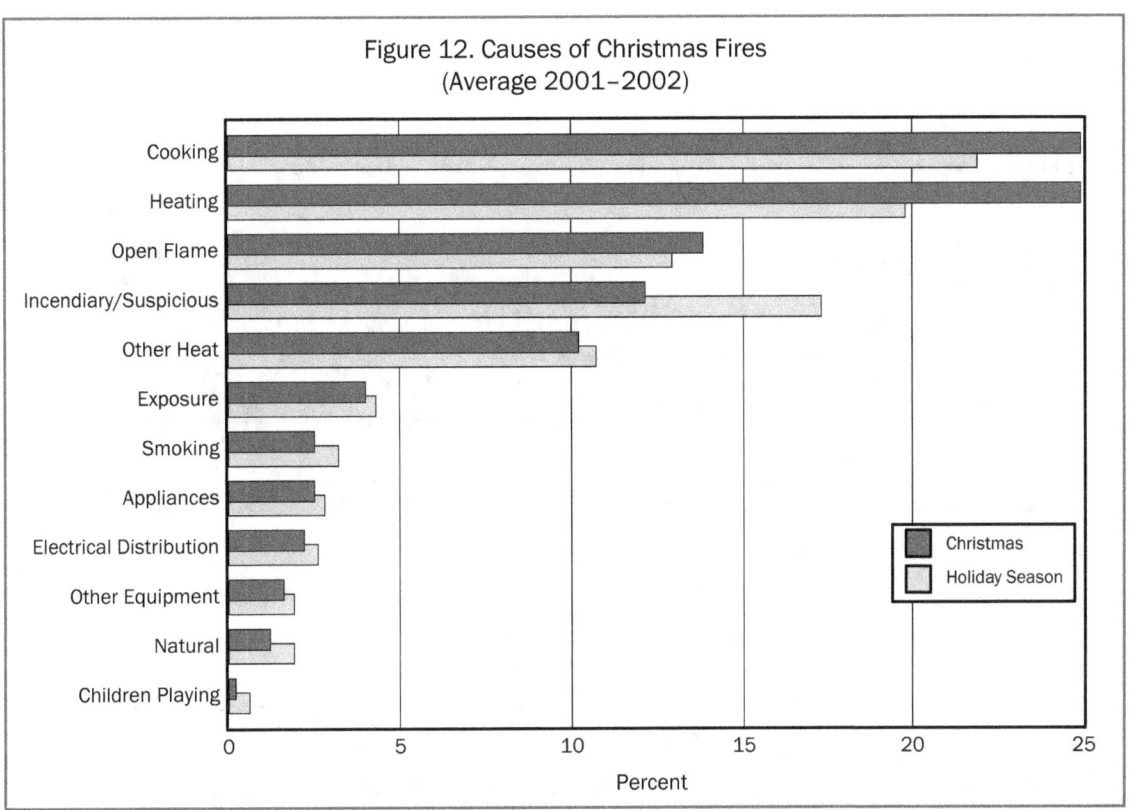

The total average dollar loss for December 24, 25, and 26 is nearly $92 million. These losses are the result of an estimated 12,600 fires requiring a fire department response. These fires are estimated to result in an average of 205 injuries and 34 fatalities. The use of alcohol and other substances may certainly play a role in increasing fire incidence during the winter holiday season. This is especially true with New Year's Eve fires, as New Year's Eve is widely celebrated with higher-than-usual consumption of alcohol. Like Christmas, the fire losses due to New Year's celebrations are high.

On December 31 and January 1, there are 55 fatalities and 160 injuries resulting from fire, and property loss is also estimated to be $92 million. Cooking is the leading cause of fires on New Year's Eve and heating is the leading cause of New Year's Day fires (Figure 14). Incendiary or suspicious fires account for 19 percent of fires on New Year's Eve and decrease to 17 percent of fires on New Year's Day, slightly below the proportion for an average holiday day.

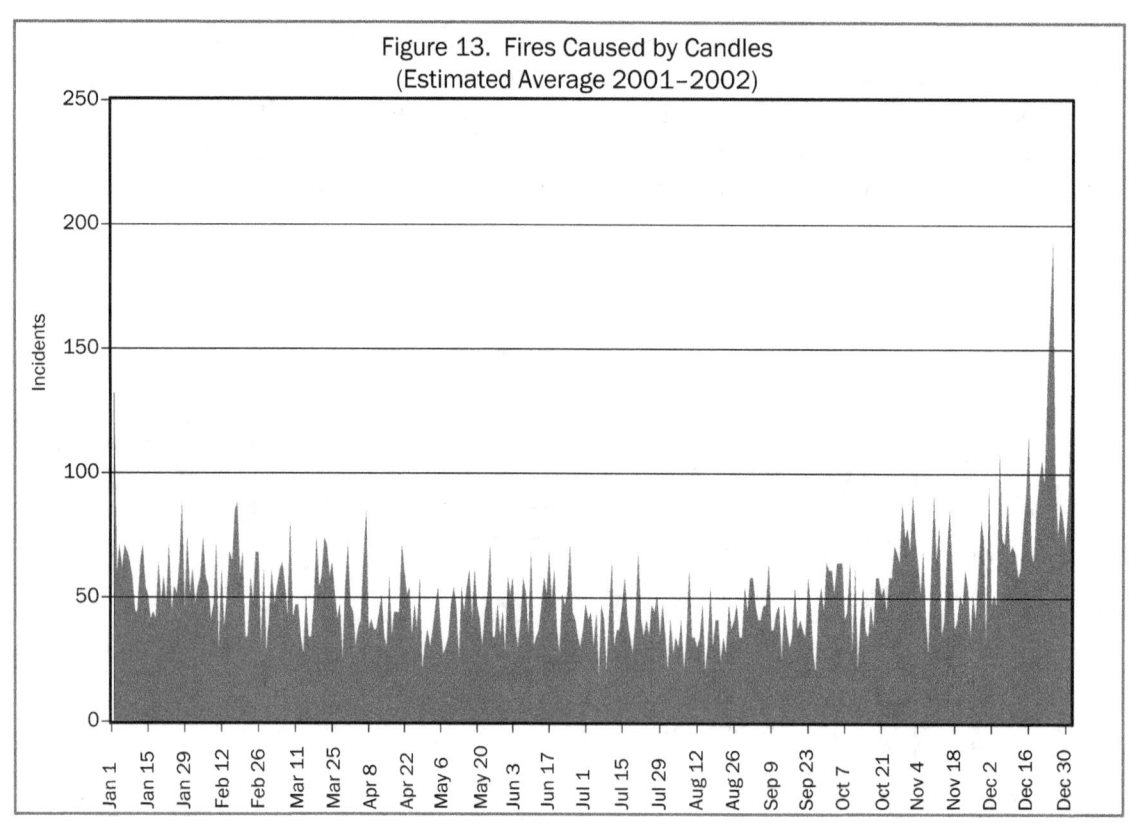

Figure 13. Fires Caused by Candles
(Estimated Average 2001–2002)

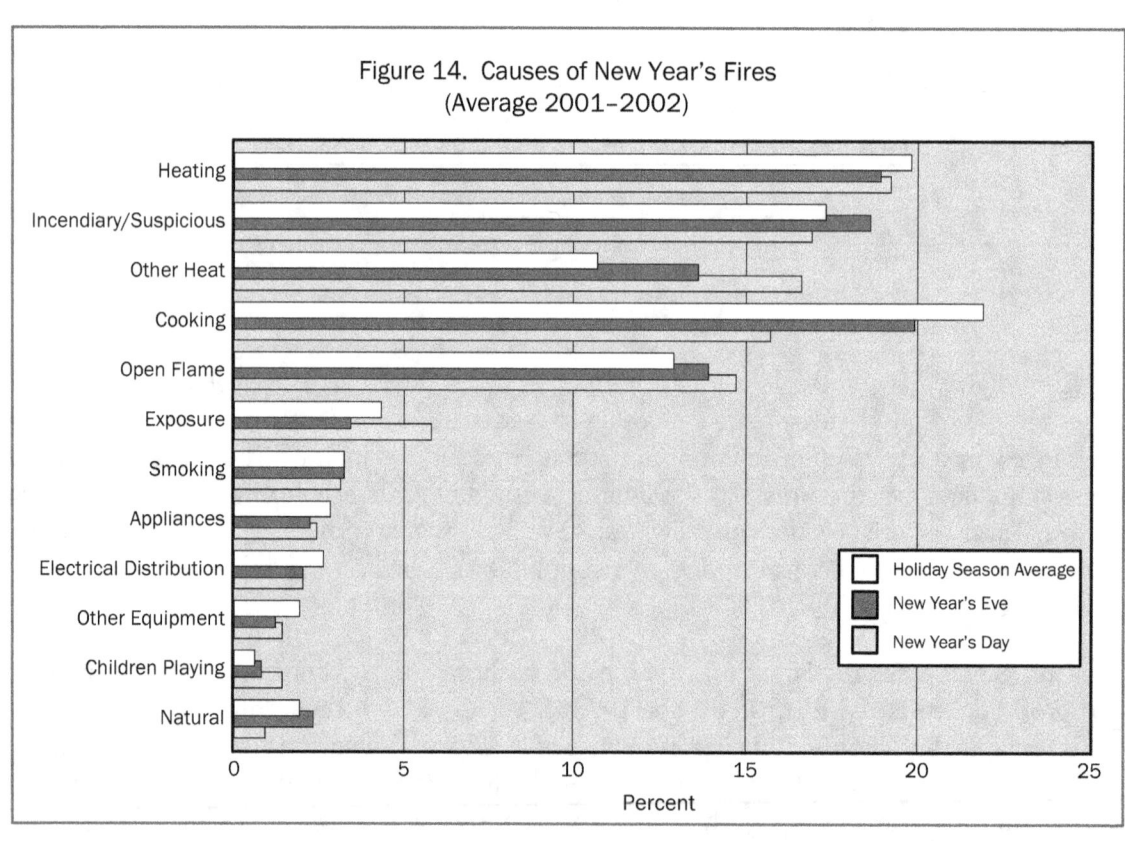

Figure 14. Causes of New Year's Fires
(Average 2001–2002)

Conclusion

Armed with an understanding of the nature and scope of seasonal fires, the fire service has the opportunity to plan and implement specific public education, fire prevention, and other fire-related programs that address seasonal changes in fire incidence. Communities are encouraged to analyze their own seasonal and holiday fire incidence to determine how prevention initiatives and programs could best be targeted. It appears that much of the seasonality of fires is due to common behaviors and causes that are repeated each year. These repetitive causes and behaviors are candidates for clearly targeted prevention initiatives and programs. Locally as well as nationally, these initiatives and programs could have a major impact on the reduction of fire incidence.